LET'S READ 6

REVISED EDITION

by

LEONARD BLOOMFIELD

and

CLARENCE L. BARNHART

ROBERT K. BARNHART

revised by

CYNTHIA A. BARNHART

Educators Publishing Service, Inc.
31 Smith Place, Cambridge, Massachusetts 02138
1-800-225-5750 www.epsbooks.com

PRINTED IN THE UNITED STATES OF AMERICA

June 2001 Printing

CONTENTS

LET'S READ 6

REVISED EDITION

LESSONS ARE NUMBERED AT THE TOP OF THE PAGE,
PAGES AT THE BOTTOM

1

bee	fee	tee
see	lee	wee

free	flee	three
tree	glee	
spree		treetop

tee	fee	fee	flee
tree	free	flee	free

tee	tree	fee	flee
fee	free	lee	glee

2

beet feet tweet greet sheet
feet fleet sweet
meet sleet street

bee sleet fee sleet
beet sweet feet fleet

feed weed deed reed
seed need heed

freed breed bleed speed weed
greed creed tweed

fee breed see feed greed
feed bleed seed feet greet

3

A bee sat on Pat's neck. Pat felt it.
When Pat struck at the bee,
it stung her.

Al fell from a tree and did not land
on his feet. Did Al bleed?

Did you see the robin
land in the treetop?
It had to flee from fleet Frank Fox.

The streets are full of sleet.
Lots of trucks slip and get stuck.
They cannot get free of the sleet.

4

deep seep sheep creep sleep
keep weep steep
peep beep sweep

see weed deep sheep creed
seep weep deed sheet creep

indeed

peek week meek creek cheek
seek leek reek Greek

weekend

wee peek meek sheep greed
week peep meet sheet Greek

5

You can creep into the shed
    and peep at Pat's sheep.
She keeps the wee sheep in the shed.

When Sid gets mud on his feet,
    he tracks it on the rug.
Sid says he will sweep it up.
I do not think he will do it.

On the weekend, Stan and Ann Meeks
    set up camp next to Weed Creek.
Stan and Ann will get up at six
    and fish. Stan gets his rod and reel.
    Ann has hers.
They will fix a lunch of fish
    from the creek.

6

feel peel reel steel wheel
heel keel eel

seen teen green sheen queen
keen screen

fifteen sixteen

beef seem leech speech tee
reef deem beech teeth
teem beechnut screech

fee	see	see	bee	bee
feel	seen	seem	beef	beech

7

Chet had fifteen beechnuts in a dish.
He will feed them to his pet chipmunk.

Frank had beef and beets and
a sweet bun. Such a lunch!
Frank must feel as if he has had a lot.

A thrush pecks at a seed.
Can it peel the husk from the seed?

The queen had a green dress.
It had a big red sash.
It must feel grand to be a queen!

8

deer peer steer cheer
beer jeer sneer
leer veer
sheer deerskin

deer jeer beer veer peer
leer peer deer leer beer

deer deep sneer
peer peep steer steel

deep peek steel reef weep
deed peel steep reel weed
deem peep sleep reed week

9

The men on a ship peer into the mist. They see a reef. The ship must veer to clear the reef. It must steer left. The men cheer when they see the ship will not meet the reef.

Can a cat sneer at a rat? Will the rat leer back at the cat?

Meg got a deep cut on her heel. Let's cheer her up!

Ted got a gift. He got deerskin mocs from his mom.

creed	greet	tweet	creep	sleet
creep	green	tweed	creek	sleep

flee	free	lee	peek	keep
fleet	reef	eel	leek	keel

see	fee	bee	lee	wee
seed	feet	beet	leek	weed
seep	feed	beef		weep
seek	feel			week

Nick will meet Dad and Sis at three.
Nick will greet Dad and Sis.

11

Dick's Cat

This week Dick Smith got a sleek cat.
It's a grand cat, but it is a scamp.
It leaps at Dick's pup. It can
run up a tree in a wink.
When the cat hid in a tree next to
the tool shed, Dick did not see it.
The cat was not in the street and not
in the beech tree. Dick felt sad.
"Dick! Dick! Fetch me the ax
from the tool shed." Dick went
to get his dad the ax.
Up on the shelf sat his cat!

12

Dick's Cat and the Chipmunk

A chipmunk hid in a treetop.
Dick's cat sat on a stump
in the sun.
The chipmunk had seen the cat
jump up and preen himself.
The cat did not think the chipmunk
had seen him, but the chipmunk had.
The chipmunk crept onto a twig.
Snap! The chipmunk fell.
The cat sprang at the chipmunk,
but it ran in a flash to its nest.
It hid in the back of the nest.
Dick's sleek cat went back to the stump
and sat on it.

13

Beth and Sal and Nell plan to spend the weekend in the hilltops.

The three will camp and fish in a creek.

They will meet at Beth's ranch and tramp to the top of a hill. They will lug a tent and a lot of stuff.

They set up camp. They plan to fish at sunup.

Nell gets up at six. Not a bit of sun can be seen. It's dank and black!

Beth peeks from the tent. Rain! Wet!

Nell, Beth, and Sal spend the weekend in the tent.

14

pea tea flea pea
sea lea peanut

bean Jean mean clean
dean lean wean

pea bean lea lean tea
sea lean flea clean pea

sea see lea lee
tea tee flea flee

15

Jean had a swim in the sea.
She swam into a bed of seaweed. Yuck!

If Dean gets sick, Mom will fix him
lean beef and hot tea.

Bring clean sheets.
Bring a clean, thick quilt.
Let's fix up the bed.

Can a pup scratch a flea on its back?
Yes, it can, but when it went to scratch,
the pup fell onto its back!

Did Jed lean on the rack and split it?
Yes, but Jed did not mean to do it.

16

eat heat neat feat
beat meat seat peat

bleat treat cheat
cleat
pleat wheat

beat eat meat peat feat
heat seat neat beat heat

bean meat cleat pea
beat mean clean peat

beat beet feet feat
meat meet beet beat

17

Jean beat Mack at jacks.
Jean and Mack do not cheat.

Dean sits on a bench and has a treat of peanuts and pop.
Dean sets three peanuts next to him on the bench.
A chipmunk hops onto the seat.
It can see the peanuts. It gets a nut. It eats the meat of the nut but not the shell.
Dean has a treat, and the chipmunk has a treat.

A sheep bleats. A duck quacks.
A hen clucks. A pig grunts.

18

beak peak weak
leak teak

bleak creak sneak streak squeak
freak speak

leak peak weak leak freak
teak speak beak bleak creak

bead lead read

beat bead leak lead bead
bead beak lead lean read

19

The Cat and the Rat

A rat sneaks a peek at a cat.
The cat spots the rat, but the cat's weak. It has been sick.
It cannot run. It must rest.
The rat squeaks and speaks, but the cat just sits.
The rat thinks the cat sleeps.
The rat jumps up on the cat's back, but it gets a shock.
The sad, weak cat jumps up. It hits at the rat. The cat has a mean sneer.
The rat streaks into its den.
The cat will rest in the sun.

20

deal	peal	veal	steal
heal	real		
meal	seal		squeal

deal	seal	meal	real	reel
peal	steal	meat	peal	peel

each	each	leach	reach
beach	reach	bleach	breach
peach	teach		preach

beach	reach	leach	leech
teach	breach	beach	beech

21

Let's eat a hot meal—not just a snack.
You fix veal chops, and I will fix
the rest.

Ring the bell! Let it peal!
We can reach Seal Beach on the bus.
Can we get seats on the bus?

Jack cannot read yet, but Miss Peach
can teach him from *Let's Read!*

Dad plants wheat and beet crops.
Will the heat kill the crops?
It can, but rain will help Dad get
a big crop of each.

22

beam gleam ream cream
seam dream scream
team cream stream
steam

sunbeam

beam team beam seam seem
ream steam beat team teem

team ream team ream
steam cream steam stream
seam creak steal seam

heap leap cheap

23

Seth got a cheap, tin gas can at a shop. The can had a split in its seam. Seth must fix it. It leaks!

Jean had a bad dream. Did Jean scream?

A deer can run and leap well.

When I get up from a nap, I need a snack. I need a sweet peach in cream. Yum! Yum!

A team of men must fix the beam in the shed. If the men do not, the shed will sag and fall in a heap.

24

east feast yeast
beast least

beast eat beast
feast east beat

leaf sheaf
heath sheath
leash

a green leaf east and west
a sheaf of wheat

25

Beth can whip the cream.
Fran and Max can each peel a peach.
Beth and Fran and Max will feast
on a peach and cream.

Pal can fetch his leash and bring it.
Pal will leap up and get the leash.
He will bring the leash to me.

A wind from the east struck a tree,
and it fell on the shed.
It did not crack the top beam of the shed
in the least, but we need
to cut up the tree.

26

ear fear hear rear tear
dear gear near sear year

spear shear clear beard
smear

deer dear sheer shear seam seem
seer sear team teem

read reed beet beat cheep cheap
feet feat
meet meat

27

Hear the pig squeal!
Hear the sheep bleat!

A man got on the bus, and sat near us in the rear.
He had a big beard and a black bag.

Next year I will help Dad shear the sheep.

Dear me! Beth got a sting on the ear. It got red.
Smear mud on it to get rid of the sting. Quick!

28

beat	seat	peat	lean
bead	seal	pea	lea
bean	sea	peak	lead
beak	seam	peal	leak
beam	steam	peach	leap
beach	stream	preach	leaf
	scream		

lea	lee	sea	see	peal	peel
leak	leek	seam	seem	real	reel

week	weak	deer	dear
peek	peak	seer	sear

29

Nan got a smear on her pink dress.
Did Nan weep? Nan felt bad,
but she did not shed a tear.

Jean will sing at the club
when it meets next year.
Mom and Dad and I will hear Jean sing.
And I will cheer. Jean can sing well!

Each year the bleak wind from the sea
will bring mist and sleet to the land.
In the spring the sun
will stream on the land.
It will clear the mist and bring
the green leaf to the treetops.

boo moo woo shoo
coo too zoo

moon soon loon spoon croon
noon boon coon swoon

spoon moon
teaspoon moonbeam

moo boo soon spoon coon
moon boon noon teaspoon croon

boo too soon
bee tee seen

31

Seth Gets the Bus

Seth must eat lunch and meet the bus
at noon.
Will Seth eat too much and miss
the bus to the zoo?
Will Seth quit and jump up to catch it?
The bus beeps. It is near!
Seth jumps up.
He sprints to the bus stop.
Seth's in luck.
He gets the bus.
But he was not a bit too soon.

32

boot toot moot scoot shoot
hoot loot

too moo boon
toot moot boot

poop loop scoop stoop troop
sloop snoop swoop droop

scoop swoop shoo scoop
stoop snoop shoot scoot

cool pool tool pool drool
fool tool stool spool

too coo tool pool drool
tool cool toot poop droop

33

Mom has to shoo the cat from the the trash can. It scoots when Mom hits the can lid.

A troop of chimps hid in the brush. Will the chimps fool the big cat who sniffs near? The chimps must be still! Soon the big cat trots to the cool pond.

An elf sat on a spool. The spool is its stool.

Bill stoops to scoop up the mess on the rug. Bill had spilt a bag of sand.

34

boom loom loom loom
doom zoom bloom gloom

boo zoo boom loom boon
boom zoom bloom loon boom

boot loom loot deem
boom loot loom doom

goof woof poof spoof proof

goof woof poof poof
poof goof spoof proof

woo poof poof spoof
woof poop pool spoon

35

A big shed and a tree stand in the gloom on a bleak heath.

A tramp sneaks up. The tramp seeks a spot to sleep.

Can the tramp stand the gloom of the shed? Its squeaks and creaks will not spook him!

The wind shifts. Poof!

It snuffs the tramp's lamp.

Bang! Boom! The split planks on the shed swing and bang in the wind.

The squeaks and gloom do spook the tramp. He jumps up and sneaks on.

36

food mood brood

moo mood food mood
mood food fool moon

booth toothbrush
tooth toothpick

too boo tooth
tooth booth teeth

boost spook

boo boot spook spoon
boot boost spool spook

37

Spot's Pups

Spot had ten pups—a big brood.
When the pups got big, Ed had to feed the pups milk and meal.
When the pups got teeth, Ed fed the pups beef and lots of meal.
Such greed! Ed got the meat in a can and the meal in a big, green bag.
Ed had to spend a lot on food, but each pup had a grand feast.
In the end, Ed had a plan.
Did Sam, Max, Nick, and Dan need a pup?
Did Jean, Fran, Beth, Liz, Ann and Sid need a pup, too?
They did and each got a free pup!

38

poor	boor	moor	spoor

poor	moor	boor	poor
boor	poor	moor	spoor

poor	boor
peer	beer

Poor Jean. Jean got a bad chill.
Jean must rest in bed and sleep.
At noon Jean can get up and eat lunch.
Jean must eat bland food—
hot mush and cream. Too bad!
Quick, Bess! Bring Jean a spoon.
Must we feed Jean? She will not eat
her mush!

39

Beth has a green toothbrush.
Mom got Beth's brush in a shop.
Beth keeps the brush in a box.
When Beth eats a meal, she will brush
and scrub each bit of food
from each tooth.
She has the best, clean teeth!

Six spooks in a mood to fool zoom
into a pool and swim. The spooks boo
at a poor gull. It swoops into a tree.
Six spooks hear a squeak and a moo!
Who is it? Six spooks
are not in a mood to fool!

40

boo	moo	loom	coo	soon
boot	moot	loot	coon	spoon
boon	moon	loon	cool	spool
boom	mood	loop		spook

fool	poop	tooth	sleep
feel	peep	teeth	sloop
feed	peel	tee	stoop
food	pool	too	steep

seen	moot	deem	brood	steel
soon	meet	doom	breed	stool

41

I am in a sloop on the sea.
I can feel the wind.
I can feel the sea rock the sloop.
I hear the hoot of a loon.
I peer at the moon.
It was a grand dream.

A man had big, black boots.
The boots left a big, black stain
on the rug.

Jean can peel the skin from a peach.
Next she can eat it!

42

Goof Spook

Goof Spook got a mop.
Goof hid in a shed.
Leech Spook peeps into the shed.
Goof squeaks "Boo!" at poor Leech.
Leech streaks from the spot.
Goof Spook jumps on the mop. Zoom!
Goof loops and swoops at Leech.
It's such a fuss when a spook
spooks a spook!

43

The Codfish Men

A ketch drifts from its fleet
in the mist on the sea.
The sea slaps on the hull,
and the planks on the deck creak.
Each man squints and can see land.
A swell lifts the ketch.
The swell sweeps the ketch
onto the rocks.
The rocks split the hull.
The gush of the sea into the hull
sinks the ketch.
The men leap into the sea.
The men cling to planks.
The codfish men drift on the planks
to a beach.

44

gain pain vain fain
main rain lain

raindrop

rain rain lain pain chain
brain train blain Spain
drain strain slain stain
grain sprain plain swain maintain

twain

brain stain train Spain plain
blain slain twain sprain pain

45

Pat's Truck

We had a big rain. Pat's truck slid into a deep drain on Main Street. Pat got a chain to drag the truck from the ditch. Next he had to clean the mud from his truck.

Did you hear the hoot of the train? It will gain speed and rush to its next stop.

Clem has a pet steer. He keeps it in a pen. The steer eats grain.

46

faint saint quaint
paint taint

pain fain faint paint
paint faint taint saint

aid maid raid staid
laid paid braid

laid maid raid
paid aid braid

laid pain raid main staid
lain paid rain maid stain

47

Pat got green stain at the shop on Main Street.
Pat and Dick must fix the big box and paint it green.
They will be paid to do the job.

Ann fell from a tree. She got a bad bump and felt faint.
Bill ran to her aid.

A chain hung in a loop on the back of a dump truck.
Will the chain bang on the truck and chip its paint?
Will the chain rust in the rain and stain the truck?

48

fail mail sail wail
hail pail tail ail
jail rail bail

rail rail snail mailbox
trail frail
brail flail quail sailfish

rail fail nail bail
trail frail snail brail
tail rail sail rail

fail main rail pain trail
fain mail rain pail train

49

See the pup wag its tail!

Tom laid the nail on the shelf.

A snail cannot run and jump.
A snail just creeps!

The mail truck will bring the mail, and Lee will get it from the mailbox.

It's fun to tramp on a trail.

If a rail has a split in it, a train can crash. The trackmen peer at the crack in the rail and fix it.

50

wait bait trait strait

wait bait trait strait
wail bail train strain

aim maim claim waif

aim maim wail waif
ail main waif wait

waist faith

waist
wait

51

Tess got a big pail of bait.
If Sam and Al each get a rod and reel, the three can fish.

Wag stuck his tail into a pail of paint.
Let's get Wag to help us paint the mailbox!

Jeff gets mad too much.
It's a bad trait.

Jack's pants had too big a waist.
He has a belt to keep the pants up.
But when Jack jumps, the pants slip from his waist.

52

air	lair	stair	chair
fair			
hair	airship	hairpin	
pair	airsick	haircut	

Jack, get a haircut! Soon!

Dad fell on the stair.
Frank ran to get Dad a chair.

A cub and its mom hid in a lair.

Mom got Pat socks at a shop.
Mom got Max a pair, too.

53

Jack's Trip

Jack went on a big trip.
He went in a jet to Spain.
Did Jack get airsick?
He had a pill,
and did not get airsick.
Will Jack send us mail from Spain?
Yes, the mail from Jack will be
in the mailbox.
Will Jack get back soon?
Jack will not get back till next spring.

aim	wait	mail	pain	rain
ail	wail	maid	pail	raid
aid	waif	main	paid	rail

twain	braid	staid	faint
train	brail	stain	fain
trail	brain	strain	fail
trait	blain		faith

Nell had fair hair, Ann had red hair,
and Bess had black hair.
Bess can fix her hair in a braid.

55

The Rain Maid

Kit ran in the rain. Such fun!
Splash mud on the feet. Splash rain on pants.
Raindrops drip from Kit's chin.
Each bit of Kit gets wet!
Rain gets Kit's hair damp.
Mom says Kit is a rain maid.
Kit thinks her Mom will not get too upset with her.
Kit will not bring in the rain.
She will not trail mud from her boots onto the stair.
Kit will just run in the clean, fresh rain.

56

bay	gay	lay	pay	way
day	hay	may	ray	
Fay	jay	nay	say	away

haystack   railway

today

hay	gay	bay	way	lay
nay	jay	pay	may	Fay
may	pay	day	ray	hay

a day in May   a railway train

Dad will meet the train at Green Bay.

57

Can an elf sit on a sun ray?

May we lift the box from the shelf?
Lift the box the way Dan did.

Help me lay the sheet on the bed.
We can stretch it and tuck it in.

On a hot day Dean lay in the hay
and slept. It's a grand way to nap.

Did Ned pay the man? Ned paid him,
and the man went away.

Hear the jay up in the tree!
Hear the jay screech and jeer!

58

ray ray ray ray
bray gray pray tray
dray pray spray stray
fray tray

lay lay way play
clay play sway plaything
flay slay stay

ray fray ray pray way sway
lay flay lay play lay slay

Bess set six cups on a tray.

Which way did the cat stray?

59

We spray the plants to feed them.
The plants get big and green from the food.

Did Fay pick up a stray pup?
Well, a stray, gray pup did pick up Fay.
It jumps up on Fay and licks her.
Fay and the pup play. It will stay and fetch a stick, a rock, a rag.
The pup eats a lot. It licks up its food. Each meal is a feast!
Soon the pup is big and plump.
Fay must keep the pup.
It is a pet, not a stray.

60

Fran and the Sheep

In the dusk and thick mist Fran and Shep cannot see the trail.

They cannot tell which will lead them and the sheep back to the ranch.

The flock will stray if they cannot stay on the trail.

Shep yaps and keeps the sheep in a bunch.

Fran can just see the trail. The ranch is near. Soon the sheep will lay in the hay in the shed.

61

Shep and the Fox

Shep can smell a fox. His hair sticks up on his back.
The fox can smell Shep, too. It slinks away and will not get a sheep.

Dan and the Haystack

Dan lay in the haystack. In his sleep he can hear faint yaps. It's Shep!
Shep jumps on Dan to get him up.
“Shep, get away!’ says Dan. But Dan gets up to stop Shep's yaps.
“Rain! It may rain,” thinks Dan.
“The hay! I must bring it in!”
Dan has to get the hay into the shed.
If it gets wet, the hay will rot.

62

boat moat float shoat oat
coat oats
goat stoat throat

sailboat steamboat oatmeal

road load toadstool railroad
toad goad

Joan moan roan
loan roan groan

oak cloak
soak croak

63

A goat leaps and bleats. It will eat coats and oats.
A toad hops and croaks. It sits on a toadstool.

When the wagon hit an oak tree, its load of hay fell on the road.
The men must pitch the hay back into the wagon.

On a cool, crisp day, Dad eats oatmeal.
Hot oatmeal and sweet cream cheer him up on a dim, bleak day, too.

Joan has a red throat. She is sick.
Do not moan and groan about it.
Stay in bed! And get well soon!

64

coal foam coax oaf
goal loam hoax loaf
foal roam

soap oath

boast roast coach roach
coast toast poach broach

cockroach

foal goal loaf roam soak
foam goat loam road soap

road roan goat moat load
roan roam goal moan loan

65

Jean can poach an egg. Bill can fix oatmeal and heat up a bit of the roast ham. I will toast the fresh loaf. We can fix a feast!

The team won! May got a goal.
The coach got us a treat!

Can we coax the foal and the goat into the pen?

The boat drifts near the coast.
We can see sea foam on the rocks.

Neal had to clean the coal bin.
He got black from the coal dust.
He must soak and soap himself clean!

66

oar	boar	board
boar	board	hoard
roar	aboard	
soar		
	blackboard	billboard

boar	boar	board
soar	board	hoard

a nail in a board   an oar and a sail

Just hear the wind roar!
See the treetops sway in the wind!
Soon it will rain.

67

Get aboard the boat, Sal,
and hand Jan an oar.

Help us get the big board up
onto the top of the shed!
Tom will help Frank and Al and me.
We can nail it to the top of the shed,
and the shed will not leak.

Joan can read well.
Joan can read from the blackboard.
Joan can read the print
on a billboard, too.
Did Joan teach herself to read?

68

pay	say	bay	Fay	way
pray	stay	bray	flay	sway
play	stray	fray	slay	

oat	coal	load	goat	foam
oak	coat	loaf	goal	foal
	coast	loam	goad	
soap		loan		moat
soak				moan

boat	coat	oat	goat
boast	coast	shoat	gloat

69

Seth's Goat

Seth's dad got him a goat.
Seth pets the goat,
but the goat jumps and butts him.
Seth picks himself up and thinks,
"The goat did not mean it."
Seth pats the goat on its neck,
but the goat jumps back.
Seth hops away and thinks,
"The goat did not mean it."
Seth steps up and pats the goat
on its back, and the goat jumps and
stamps in the mud.
"A goat butts and kicks and stamps.
A goat just cannot play! A goat
is a goat, not a pet!"

70

out lout tout pout
bout rout gout

outlet outfit about
outset outwit

scout spout trout clout shout
snout sprout flout
stout

ouch couch slouch
couch crouch
pouch grouch

mouth south

71

King Max and the Red Hat

King Max had a red, felt hat.
King Max went out in the rain.
The fresh, clean rain soaks
his red, felt hat.
It drips red drops!
Soon King Max was a red king.
He had a red cloak and a red hand
and red hair.
Poor King Max!
Just a neat, felt hat in the rain
paints a king red.
Groan! Groan! King Max must get
a haircut and a clean outfit.
A king cannot slouch on his couch and
pout about a bad day!

72

bound mound sound round
found pound wound ground
hound round

around playground unwound
roundup background

count mount fount

loud proud shroud foul
cloud

mound fount lout cloud
mount found loud clout

73

Hank's hound pup bit him. Ouch!

Let's not sit on the wet ground.
Let's run on the playground.

Dad wound the clock and set it at ten.

Jim can count out loud.

A chipmunk sits on a mound of nuts.
See the chipmunk pick up a nut
and stuff it in its mouth!
Its round cheeks puff out.
The chipmunk has got a pouch
in its mouth!

74

our sour dour flour scour

Jim must scour the pan to clean it.

If Jill keeps the milk cool,
it will not sour.

The Rain Cloud

See the big, black cloud in the south!
Feel the wind! Soon it will rain.
Quick, let's run!
Let's not get wet.
Let's not stay out in the rain.
Let's play in the shed.

75

The Pup and the Toad

Our hound pup found a toad
on the ground.
Our hound pup did not snap
at the toad.
Our pup just sat still
and let the toad hop.
It just let the toad hop around
on the ground.

The Trout Stream

Clem will fish in the stream.
Clem may get a trout.
If Clem can just get a trout,
Mom will fix it, and he will eat it
at lunch.

76

The Seal

Did you see the seal at the zoo?
The seal did tricks.
Did a man train the seal?
Yes, he fed the seal a fish
when the seal did a trick.
Did the man fling a fish at the seal?
Yes, and the seal will catch it
in its mouth.
The seal can snatch the fish
from the air!
A seal can catch fish well!

77

Goat Tricks

A man had a goat.
He had to load his goat into a truck.
But the goat had a fear of trucks.
The man got a stick to goad the goat.
The goat got the stick and had a meal of it.
The way to get the goat into the truck is to feed it oats and hay.
If the man sets oats and hay on a ramp into the truck, the goat will eat his way up the ramp.
And the man can get the goat into his van.

78

bow how mow row sow
cow now Dow wow

cowshed haymow

row	row		cow	
brow	prow	plow	scow	chow

owl fowl jowl growl
cowl howl yowl scowl prowl

cow	how	row	row
scow	howl	prow	prowl
scowl	fowl	brow	growl

79

Hear the cow moo!
Hear the owl hoot!
Hear the fox growl!
Hear the hound howl at the moon!
Hear each sound around you!

Bow-wow! Hear Shep howl and growl at the fox in the cowshed.
The fox is on the prowl to get a fowl.
How can a poor fox eat if Shep sets up such a row?

It is spring now, and Dow must plow and plant.

80

down gown town

uptown downtown

brown drown clown
crown frown

down brown clown
Dow brow crown

Let's not frown and sulk
and grouch around. Let's get out
in the fresh air and play.

Uptown! Downtown!
Run around the town!

81

The brown owl is a clown. It hops up and down on its branch. It leaps into the air.

It swoops down to the ground to snatch up its food.

It can growl and hoot. It can just sit and blink. It can seem to sleep.

Each day Bess gets up at six and milks our brown cow, May.

Bess milks the cow out in the cowshed.

She sets the pail down on the ground to catch the milk. It has foam on it.

When Bess milks our cow, May lets out a moo of thanks.

jaw paw saw daw
law raw caw maw

outlaw seesaw

claw craw thaw
flaw draw
slaw straw Shaw

law saw law raw caw
claw slaw claw draw craw
caw law craw daw raw
raw

raw row raw mow
saw sow draw Dow

83

Frank Shaw can draw well.
Frank will draw a big ship—
a sloop at sail on the sea.

I saw a jackdaw in a tree. It had
a bit of straw in its claw. Maybe
it had to fix its nest.
The jackdaw had such a loud caw!

In the spring the sun will thaw
the ground, and each tree
and shrub will bloom.

To fix meatloaf, you need raw beef.
But it must be ground up raw beef.

84

awl brawl crawl shawl
bawl crawl scrawl
pawl trawl sprawl
yawl

dawn lawn yawn draw pawn
fawn pawn drawn brawn spawn

paw awl draw bawl
pawl yawl drawl brawl
pawn yawn drawn brawn

hawk squawk

85

It's cool out on the lawn.
Jeff, run and fetch me a shawl.
Get the brown shawl.

A deer can run and jump and leap.
A cat can creep and crawl.
A hawk can swoop and soar.
A cow can munch and moo.
A sheep can trot and bleat.

Squawk! A hawk swoops down to get at the hen and her chicks.
Get the drum, Tom. Bang on it!
Shoo away the hawk!
Do not let the hawk grab the hen and the chicks.

86

haul Paul fault
maul Saul

launch paunch staunch
haunch

haunt gaunt flaunt
taunt jaunt
daunt vaunt

taut

taut haunt haunch
taunt

87

"Help! Help!" Did May hear a shout?
Yes, she did. It was Paul. He fell into the pond, but May found him.
Paul did not drown. May got him out.

How can Saul eat a lot and not get a paunch? Saul must just need to eat.

Jean and Joan went on a jaunt in a launch.

Nat will not sleep in the hut.
He thinks a spook haunts it.
Pat speaks up and says, "Let's not let a spook daunt us. Let's haunt the spook!"

cow	caw	owl	awl
sow	saw	yowl	yawl

draw	bawl
drawn	brawl
brawn	brawn

mound	found	out	loud
mount	fount	ouch	lout

awl	daw	paw	taut
shawl	draw	law	taunt
shaw	drawn	lawn	jaunt

89

Mom and Jean and Will left at dawn.

They went on a hunt to see deer and hawks and muskrats and maybe an owl.

They see a hawk swoop in the air.

A jay taunts the hawk. It has a loud caw.

When Mom and Jean and Will sat down to eat lunch, they saw a deer and a fawn. The fawn got milk from its mom and lay down near her.

She had a bit of lunch and let her fawn sleep.

Mom and Jean and Will say the hunt was the best one yet!

90

boy Roy coy
joy toy soy

cloy Troy

cowboy

coy Roy boy
cloy Troy cowboy

Dad got Roy a toy train.
The train ran on a round track.
It ran round and round and round.
Toot, toot! Whiz! Swish!

91

Joy saw Troy snatch Jack's cowboy hat. Troy kept the hat and ran away.

Skip, Jack's hound pup, saw Troy run with Jack's hat. He ran.

When a pup spots a boy on the run, the pup thinks it must run, too.

It must catch up and play.

Troy ran from Skip. He did not wish to get a nip from the pup.

Skip did catch up to Troy. He lept up to get Jack's hat.

Troy let Skip get the hat.

Thanks to Skip, Jack got back his cowboy hat.

92

oil coil toil boil soil
boil soil foil broil spoil

coin loin groin
join

joint moist hoist
point foist joist

oil boil join coin
foil broil joint coil

topsoil pinpoint
uncoil standpoint

93

The Owl

"See the big owl up in the tree!"
Fran saw the owl and Sal saw the owl,
  but Tom and Bill did not see it.
"Point at it, Fran. Point it out,
  and Tom and Bill will see it, too."
The owl still sat up in the tree.
"Hoot, hoot, hoot!" went the owl.
When Tom and Bill did hear
  the owl, they saw it, too.

Mom will boil the meat
  and loop foil around it.
The foil will keep the meat moist.

goose	geese	least	coarse
loose			hoarse
moose		grease	
noose		crease	

A goose, a duck, a chick, a hawk, and an owl can each lay an egg.
A fox will steal a goose egg.

A moose eats coarse straw and hay.

A pot of grease fell from the shelf.
The cat dips her paw into the pot.
She licks the grease from each crease in her paw.

95

Bill Fox is an outlaw.
He will steal a chicken in a wink.
Kep Hound is a lawman.
He will get Bill one day!

Bill thinks he can coax a chick out of the shed. He will snatch it up and stuff it in his pouch.
But Mom Hen has a cool plan.
She and Kep the Lawman will sit in a big box to wait for Bill.

Bill creeps up to steal a chick.
Mom Hen sets up a coarse screech.
Kep Hound sets up a yowl.
Bill ran away, and he will stay away.
He thinks spooks are in the shed.

house douse louse
mouse souse

louse grouse spouse
blouse

dollhouse henhouse bunkhouse
playhouse hothouse clubhouse

sense dense tense manse rinse

else pulse

copse apse glimpse
lapse

97

Fluff, our cat, got a mouse,
but not in our house.
Fluff got a big, brown mouse
in the henhouse next door.

The mist is dense on the sea.
Tom is tense at the helm
of his sailboat.
He cannot get a glimpse of the rocks
he thinks are near.
He must just sail on. He cannot
do much else.

Tess got grease on Beth's blouse.
She must rinse out the grease spot
and press the blouse.

98

breeze sneeze squeeze wheeze freeze

gauze adze axe

It's cool now. Feel the cool breeze.
Hear Tom sneeze!
Tom must not stay out. He will get sick. Tom will get hoarse and wheeze.

The wind will yowl and howl.
Soon the pond will freeze.
It will not thaw until spring.

99

Dick got up at dawn and went out. He saw a deer and a fawn. They saw Dick and ran away from him. They hid. Dick saw a hawk. Hawks steal chicks. Dick had to run. He cannot let the hawk get his chicks.

Dick got the hen and the chicks into the henhouse and shut it up. The chicks hid in the straw. The hen sat on top of the chicks! The hawk went away.

Roy cut himself on an axe.
Quick! Rinse the cut! Clean it!
Get help! Get the gauze! Fix the cut!

100

have peeve leave twelve

weave

give sleeve shelve

live delve

bade groove solve

Each board had a groove in it.

Ann can weave. Ann has a loom.

A cow can give a big pail of milk.

Let's have lunch at twelve.
Let's have a big lunch!

101

Stan and Jean live in the manse on the hill. Each day Stan and Jean leave the manse and play at Jack's house. At twelve they have lunch.

Jeb saw a bug weave a web.

Nan got grease on Pat's coat.
It's a big spot on the sleeve.
It will peeve Pat. Poor Nan!

Six and ten are sixteen.
Can you solve six and three?

A seal sits on a rock. It waits to catch a fish.
It will give the fish to its pup.

boy	bay	Roy	ray	Roy
joy	jay	soy	say	Troy

boil	bail	soil	sail
toil	tail	foil	fail

rin	man	moo	ten	lap
rinse	manse	moose	tense	lapse

free	lea	ad	ax	bad
freeze	leave	adze	axe	bade

Pam may pick up the pup,
but Pam must not squeeze it.
The pup will squeal.

103

A Wet Cat

Sis saw a cat in a tree near the pond.
The cat hit at a bug.
Flip-flop, the bug and the cat fell into the pond. Can Sis fish the cat out on a stick? The cat cannot swim.
Can Paul help haul him out?
If the cat can grab the stick and stay on, Paul and Sis can hoist it from the pond.
Will the cat stay still and hang on to the stick? Paul and Sis lift the cat out. When the cat's on land, it jumps from the stick.
It's wet and mad, mad, mad.

104

At Camp

Each year Seth's dad and three men hunt deer at a camp in Green Bay.

Seth's dad and the three men hunt quail and duck, too. They sleep on cots in a big tent. At six the men get up and fix hot tea and oatmeal and toast.

Each year Seth's dad gets a deer, a duck, a quail, and a bad chill.

Seth's dad may stay in bed a week from the chill.

A cat will catch a mouse.

A fox will steal a goose.

A bat will swoop down to catch insects in the air.

105

Jack and Al in a Boat

Jack and Al went out on the pond
in a boat.
"Sit still, Jack! The boat will rock."
But Jack did not sit still in the boat.
"Sit still, Jack! The boat will tip!"
But Jack did not sit still.
The boat did tip a bit,
and Jack fell out.
Jack fell into the pond. Splash!
"Help! Help! Get me out!"
Al held out an oar.
"Grab the oar, Jack!"

(See about Jack on 116)

106

(Jack and Al in a Boat)

Jack cannot grab the oar.
Jack cannot help himself.
See Jack thrash! Al can swim well.
Al jumps in and gets Jack.
Al helps Jack back up on land.

From the bank, Meg saw how Jack fell into the pond.
She saw Al haul him out.
It's Jack's fault.
Jack just cannot sit still.
But now Jack will at least sit still in a boat.

The End

107

Pat and the Bus

Pat scoots down the street.
Can Pat catch the bus?
Not if Pat slips on the wet street.
Pat slips. Bump!
A man stops and helps Pat.
Pat gets up and limps on.
Pat and the man get up the hill
just when the bus stops.
Pat thanks the man and gets on.
Pat drops a coin in the slot
and sits down in a seat.
Now Pat can rest.

108

A Feast

It's twelve! It's noon! Let's eat! I can eat a house! I can eat a pail of food! Let's not wait to fix lunch. Let's do it now!

We will have the best food. You and I can have a muffin and toast and egg and ham and pop and tea and milk and chips and franks and veal loaf and roast beef and cream and peach and plum jam on a bun.

Well, maybe we can wait until twelve-fifteen, and Sis and Bob and Mom can help us fix such a grand feast.

109

The Sailboat

Dad got Fran a big toy sailboat.
"Let's see it sail."
"Let's sail the boat on the pond."
Fran set the boat on the pond,
and away it went.
See the boat sail!
When the wind hits the big sail,
the boat just scoots!
See it skim on the pond.
The boat will not tip,
and it will not sink.
It will just sail on the pond
in the wind.

110

The Hawk and the Boy

A brown hawk sits in a crag of rocks. The hawk waits, and soon it spots a rat way down on the rocks.

Swoosh! The hawk swoops down on the rat. Can the rat run away from the keen hawk?

The boy can see the hawk soar and swoop down to the ground. The boy can see the rat. He must help it.

The boy picks up a stick. He shouts at the hawk.

The hawk can see the boy and hear him shout. The rat scoots into a crack in the rocks. The boy can hear the hawk scream and screech. It cannot catch the rat now.